YOUR
TALENT
GUIDE

Your Talent Guide
Copyright © 2025 by Josefine Campbell & Gitte Justesen

All rights reserved under the Pan-American and International Copyright Conventions. This book may not be reproduced in whole or in part, except for brief quotations embodied in critical articles or reviews, in any form or by any means, electronic or mechanical, including photocopying, recording, or by any information storage and retrieval system now known or hereinafter invented, without written permission of the publisher.

ISBN (paperback): 978-1-968919-06-1
ISBN (ebook): 978-1-968919-07-8

Armin Lear Press, Inc.
215 W Riverside Drive, #4362
Estes Park, CO 80517

YOUR TALENT GUIDE

DON'T WORK AGAINST YOURSELF—
USE WHAT COMES NATURALLY

JOSEFINE CAMPBELL & GITTE JUSTESEN

CONTENTS

Find Your Sound in Life's Big Moments	1
Composing a work life that resonates	5
The 38 Talents	11
The 12 Thinking Talents	13
The 10 Striving Talents	39
The 6 Influencing Talents	61
The 6 Relating Talents	75
The Four Archetypes	89
The Four Hidden Talents	97
Understanding Talent Combinations, or Chords	113
The Power of a Shared Sound	123
Coach yourself – take small steps	129
Closing the Phrase—Not the Song	133
Appendix 1: Examples of Strengthening Chords	135
About the Authors	209

FIND YOUR SOUND IN LIFE'S BIG MOMENTS

There are moments in life when the tempo changes.

A new role.

A new team.

A goodbye.

A beginning.

In these transitions, we're invited to pause, and tune in. Who am I now? What kind of work resonates with me? Where do I belong next?

This handbook will help you listen for your own sound. Not the loudest voice in the room. Not what's trending. But the deeper notes—your natural talent chords.

Like music, your talents follow patterns. Some are strong and instinctive. Others are quiet, but useful. And a few fall outside your range, and that's okay. Knowing which is which helps you make wise decisions about how you use your time, energy, and career.

As coaches, we've worked with leaders and teams across industries, countries, and turning points. And through it all, one thing has stayed true: the most powerful shifts happen when people reconnect with their natural strengths—their own sound.

We created this guide as a tool for those moments. Not when everything is going smoothly, but when life calls for clarity. A change in job, a shift in role, or a pause to ask: Where do I go from here? How do I stay true to myself while doing it?

We're not just practitioners of talent work, we're also humans who've had to make real choices. We've both stood at career crossroads. We've both rebuilt after change.

This handbook reflects our experience as coaches and as people who believe in self-leadership, clarity, and making the most of the time we're given. If you have completed a TT38® Talent test[1], you can use this book to continue exploring your talent profile. If you have not taken the test, we encourage you to get one done. It can be your starting point for reflection.

We hope it helps you tune in to your own chord.

And lead from there.

—GITTE & JOSEFINE

---

1   Offered by Talents Unlimited, the TT38® Talent Test is based on modern strength-based research in positive psychology. The test has 440 questions and takes about 30 minutes to complete.

COMPOSING A WORK LIFE THAT RESONATES

Each talent will show up in your test profile as one of the following:
- Thinking talents help you reflect, analyze, and make sense of complexity.
- Relating talents help you connect, empathize, and create belonging.
- Influencing talents help you lead, express, and move others forward.
- Striving talents help you act, focus, and drive things to completion.

Just as in music, not every note in your range is meant to lead the melody. Some chords flow effortlessly. Others require more effort, or even leave you feeling out of tune. That's the beauty of understanding your talent profile: it helps you choose wisely where to invest your energy.

TOP TALENTS – YOUR STRONG, NATURAL CHORDS

These are your core strengths. They show up consistently, with energy and ease. When you use a top talent, you often feel more alive, more yourself. These are the talents where you can stay in flow for hours, and still leave with something in the tank.

Using a top talent typically costs half the energy of one hour spent. So, one hour spent only costs you half an hour of your personal energy. That means more sustainability, less stress, and higher-quality output.

MID TALENTS – YOUR WORKABLE, SUPPORTING NOTES

These talents are available to you, but they don't carry the same natural energy. Here you'll experience that one hour will cost you up to three hours of your personal energy. You can use them when needed, and sometimes quite well. But they require more focus and more recovery. Overusing them can feel tiring, even if the work is in your "zone."

Mid talents are useful, especially when combined with a top talent, but they're not where you'll thrive long-term. Mid talents can be **moved up if you start using them. But it takes practice.**

NON-TALENTS – QUIET STRINGS

These talents sit low in your profile. They may drain you, bore you, or frustrate you. That doesn't mean you can't work around them. But using non-talents regularly tends to lead to fatigue, stress, or underperformance—especially if you're expected to use them like strengths. This because one hour spend will cost you 6-9 hours of personal energy use.

Non-talents aren't flaws. They're signals; this might not be your stage. The more aware you are of them, the better you can set boundaries, collaborate smartly, or design roles that protect your energy.

When you know your full range, you don't waste energy pretending. You choose the chords that truly fit, and build a career that resonates. It helps you shape a working life that feels like you. One that doesn't fight your rhythm but plays in harmony with it.

WHEN THE CHORD SHIFTS, TUNE IN

As said above, this guide is especially helpful in life's pivotal moments, when you:

- Change direction in your career
- Step into a new leadership role
- Move between teams
- Rebuild after being let go
- Or simply want to reconnect with your core.

Let this be your reflection space. A way to stay close to your sound, so you can lead, grow, and choose with clarity.

You don't have to play every note. Just the ones that are truly yours.

In the next part we'll dive into the 38 talents.

THE 38 TALENTS

Here you'll get a deep dive into the understanding of each talent. First, you'll explore the 34 visible talents that appear in your talent graph and, at the end, you'll get insight into the 4 hidden talents. We call them *notes*.

THE 12 THINKING TALENTS

1. ANALYZING

What it can do

This talent enables you to see truth through evidence. You value logic, seek factual accuracy, and are great at identifying inconsistencies. You help your team make decisions based on reality—not assumptions.

In the workplace

You might be the one in a leadership meeting who says, "Let's validate that with data before we act." You are often the person who picks apart a business case or detects inconsistencies in a presentation. You create confidence when decisions are complex, because others trust your critical eye.

Example: Sofie, a head of operations, uses her analyzing talent to detect a pattern of late deliveries. Others assumed it was just seasonal. Her insight led to a deeper analysis, which exposed a bottleneck in the approval workflow.

Watch out for
Your desire for accuracy can slow progress if you always want "one more report" before moving. In fast-paced settings, this may frustrate others who are more action-oriented.

Some may also experience you as overly skeptical or critical, especially if they lead with enthusiasm or vision.

Coaching tip
Ask yourself, "when is "good enough" good enough?" Try naming your concern, then ask others if further analysis is truly needed, or if momentum matters more.

2. VISIONARY

What it can do

You instinctively see what's possible, not just what is. You imagine better futures and create excitement about new directions. This talent is especially powerful in strategy, innovation, transformation, and leadership roles where change is needed.

In the workplace

You often bring the "Why not?" energy. You speak about purpose, long-term goals, or how a current change connects to something bigger. Others might find your ideas inspiring, especially when people are stuck in short-term problems.

Example: Jamal, a divisional leader, uses his visionary talent to pitch a new go-to-market strategy that doesn't yet exist in the industry. His team is nervous, but his ability to paint the "what could be" helps them believe and align.

Watch out for
You may get ahead of others—especially those who prefer structure or stability. Your thinking might seem abstract if you don't ground it. In teams, some may think you're "dreaming" while they're "doing."

Coaching tip
Pair your vision with a tangible first step. Ask a trusted peer, "What part of this idea feels exciting, and what part feels unclear or unrealistic?"

3. HOLISTIC

What it can do

You see systems and relationships. You are attuned to purpose, values, and the interconnectedness of people, ideas, and outcomes. This makes you valuable in cultural transformation, sustainability, coaching, and stakeholder work.

In the workplace

You often connect the dots that others miss. You may ask, "How does this impact the bigger picture?" or "What's the underlying pattern here?" You're drawn to projects where alignment matters more than speed. Others might see you as intuitive or even philosophical.

Example: Lina, a senior Human Resources (HR) leader, stops a reorganization plan to point out that the proposed structure undermines the company's stated Diversity, Equity, and Inclusion (DEI) values. She links strategy, structure, and culture in a way others hadn't seen.

Watch out for

You may find it hard to prioritize when you perceive that "everything is connected." You might frustrate more task-oriented colleagues by shifting conversations to broader meaning or long-term consequences when they want to act.

Coaching tip

Before you speak, ask: Is this the right moment to zoom out? Partner with someone more execution-focused to co-balance vision and delivery.

4. INNOVATIVE

What it can do

You challenge the status quo. You enjoy thinking in new ways and generating fresh ideas—especially when something feels outdated, inefficient, or stale. You bring creative energy into teams and spark breakthrough thinking.

Example: In a product review, Lisa suggested combining two features in a completely new way, leading to a solution that differentiated the product from competitors.

In the workplace

You're often the person who says, "What if we tried this instead?" You energize idea generation, question defaults, and enjoy solving problems creatively.

Watch out for

You may struggle with repetition or get bored when there's no room for novelty. Others might feel overwhelmed by the constant flow of ideas you bring, disrupted by constant changes or unsure how to implement your ideas.

Example: During an internal process review, you proposed a complete overhaul—leaving others overwhelmed and resistant instead of inspired.

Coaching tip

Ask yourself: Who needs to come with me for this idea to land, and how can I frame it in their language?

5. CO-ORDINATING

What it can do

You bring people, tasks, and processes together with ease. You intuitively organize, align roles, and ensure progress. Others often look to you in complex situations because you see what needs to happen and make it happen.

Example: In a multi-country rollout, Thomas set up clear responsibilities and regular checkpoints, ensuring smooth collaboration and a successful launch.

In the workplace

You take initiative in bringing structure to the team. You help meetings stay focused, projects stay on track, and people stay connected to purpose and tasks.

Watch out for

You may take over too much or feel responsible for everyone's follow-through. Others may rely on you to carry the project instead of building ownership.

Example: You reorganize the team's project plan alone after one delay—while your colleagues disengage further.

Coaching tip

Ask yourself: Where can I invite others to co-own the process, rather than just follow it?

6. INQUIRING

What it can do

You love to learn. You ask questions that deepen understanding and bring curiosity to both ideas and people. You enjoy exploring new topics, tools, or trends and often become the knowledge source in your team.

Example: During a tech upgrade, Maria dove into the new system, asked smart questions, and became the informal expert others turned to.

In the workplace

You're energized by discovery. You read between the lines, ask "why," and help others stay open to learning, especially in change and transformation.

Watch out for

You may overanalyze or delay decisions in pursuit of more knowledge. Others might feel stuck if you always need more information before acting.

Example: In a hiring decision, you requested another round of interviews because you "weren't quite ready" thereby slowing the process unnecessarily.

Coaching tip

Ask yourself: What's the one thing I already know that's enough to move forward now?

7. RESEARCHING

What it can do

You go deep. You uncover insights through thorough investigation and fact-finding. Whether studying customer behavior or industry trends, you enjoy building a strong knowledge base to support smart decisions.

Example: When preparing for a client meeting, Andreas reviewed market data and internal performance history—uncovering a trend that reframed the entire proposal.

In the workplace

You bring credibility and depth. You support teams with data, documents, and well-informed viewpoints. Others trust you to back ideas with substance.

Watch out for

You may get stuck in research mode or resist action before the picture feels complete.

Example: You spent weeks building a detailed report only to realize the team needed a simpler summary earlier on to act.

Coaching tip

Ask yourself: "Is this the time to explore or to contribute what I've already found?"

8. JUST

What it can do

You care about fairness. You uphold ethical standards and ensure decisions are consistent and principled. Others often turn to you when something feels off or when a judgement call needs integrity.

Example: When two departments clashed over recognition, Amalie stepped in, not to take sides, but to propose a fair, value-driven way forward.

In the workplace

You bring a moral backbone. You challenge double standards, ask for transparency, and help the team align actions with values.

Watch out for

You may come across as rigid or overly focused on what's "right," especially when others are focused on speed or relationships.

Example: You blocked a last-minute change in a client contract, even though it could have been a smart business compromise.

Coaching tip

Ask yourself: What matters most here: the principle, the relationship, or the outcome?

9. CONTEXTUAL

What it can do
You see the bigger picture through time. You think in terms of history, past experiences, and background knowledge. You help teams avoid repeating mistakes and understand how things came to be.

Example: When a team suggested a new pricing model, Jakob reminded them of a similar one that failed five years ago and offered insights to avoid the same pitfalls.

In the workplace
You add perspective. You help people see cause and effect, trace changes over time, and build on what's already known.

Watch out for

You may dwell too much in the past or resist new approaches that lack precedent.

Example: You questioned a new team structure because "it didn't work back then"—even though the context had changed.

Coaching tip

Ask yourself: Is this past lesson still valid or is it time for a new pattern?

10. STRATEGIC

What it can do

You think in pathways. You instinctively scan for options, weigh scenarios, and choose direction with purpose. You bring clarity in ambiguity and help others move from idea to action.

Example: Faced with declining engagement, Julie proposed a three-phase retention plan that anticipated obstacles and mobilized the right stakeholders in advance.

In the workplace

You cut through complexity. You align decisions with long-term goals and help teams choose wisely, not just quickly.

Watch out for

You may over-plan or struggle when others expect flexibility or quick fixes.

Example: You delayed a launch to perfect a plan, when 80 percent readiness would've been enough to learn and adjust.

Coaching tip

Ask yourself: What's the minimum structure needed to start, and adapt as we go?

11. REFLECTIVE

What it can do

You process deeply. You pause to think, connect ideas, and form insights before speaking. Your strength lies in bringing thoughtful perspective that others miss in the rush.

Example: After a workshop, Mikkel shared a quiet but sharp observation that shifted the team's understanding of a client's need.

In the workplace

You bring depth and calm. You help teams slow down, ask better questions, and learn from experience.

Watch out for

You may appear disengaged or miss chances to contribute in fast-paced discussions.

Example: In a strategy meeting, you had a valuable insight, but didn't share it until asked, after the decision had been made.

Coaching tip

Ask yourself: What reflection is ready to be spoken, and who needs to hear it now?

12. ASSESSING

What it can do

You weigh options with care. You bring critical thinking to decisions, judging pros and cons before committing. Others rely on you to help evaluate risks, ideas, or actions before committing.

Example: Ahead of a vendor change, Freja raised three overlooked questions that helped the team avoid hidden costs.

In the workplace

You act as a filter. You help others make smarter choices by bringing balance, critique, and measured thinking.

Watch out for

You may over-assess and hesitate to act or seem negative when trying to help.

Example: Your detailed list of concerns unintentionally killed the energy in a team brainstorming session.

Coaching tip

Ask yourself: How can I assess constructively—without slowing momentum?

THE 10 STRIVING TALENTS

13. PROMINENT

What it can do

You like to be seen. You step forward with presence and confidence, often becoming the visible face of a project or team. You take the stage naturally and energize others through your drive and ambition.

Example: During a leadership summit, Emil volunteered to present the group's findings and delivered with clarity and impact.

In the workplace

You often take initiative publicly. You influence others through visibility and motivate others by showing what's possible.

Watch out for

You may seek the spotlight too often or overlook quieter voices.

Example: You dominated the discussion in a group setting, leaving little space for others to contribute.

Coaching tip

Ask yourself: Where can I share the spotlight to lift others while still being visible?

14. RESPONSIBLE

What it can do

You take ownership. You naturally feel accountable for what you commit to. Often stepping in to help or protect what matters. Others trust you because you follow through, even under pressure.

Example: When a colleague dropped out of a key task, Lotte picked it up without being asked—ensuring delivery didn't stall.

In the workplace

You're seen as reliable and dependable. You hold a strong inner standard for getting things done right.

Watch out for

You may take on too much or feel guilty when you can't fix everything. Perhaps you stay late regularly, solving issues that were never yours to begin with.

Coaching tip

Ask yourself: What's truly mine to carry, and what's not?

15. ORDERLY

What it can do

You bring clarity through structure. You prefer plans, routines, and clear expectations. You create stability and consistency in fast-moving or messy environments.

Example: Peter introduced a simple weekly checklist that helped the whole team reduce errors and stress.

In the workplace

You keep things running smoothly. You value punctuality, processes, and well-defined roles and deliverables.

Watch out for

You may become rigid or resist change that disrupts your structure.

Example: You objected to a new tool rollout because the current one "works". Even though the change could improve collaboration.

Coaching tip

Ask yourself: Where does structure support flow, and where might it block it?

16. TROUBLE-SHOOTER

What it can do

You fix things fast. You're naturally drawn to problems and motivated to find practical solutions. You stay calm under pressure and act when others hesitate.

Example: During a system outage, Jonas quickly identified the root cause and coordinated a temporary fix—minimizing downtime.

In the workplace

You're often the one people call when something breaks. You bring logic, action, and calm in critical moments.

Watch out for

You may focus too much on quick fixes and overlook root causes or strategic thinking.

Example: You solved a recurring issue again without exploring how to prevent it permanently.

Coaching tip

Ask yourself: What does this situation need; speed or sustainability?

17. FLEXIBLE

What it can do

You adapt quickly. You shift gears when needed, stay open to new input, and thrive in environments with constant change.

Example: When the client changed the scope mid-project, Sarah calmly restructured the timeline and helped the team adjust, without drama.

In the workplace

You're a stabilizer during change. Others feel safer because you don't resist what's happening—you help them adjust.

Watch out for

You may become too accommodating or unclear in your direction. Others might feel unsure of your stance.

Example: You adjusted the team's priorities several times based on feedback, until no one knew what the focus really was.

Coaching tip

Ask yourself: What needs to stay flexible, and what needs to be firm right now?

18. FOCUSED

What it can do

You concentrate deeply. You lock into a task, goal, or topic and stay there, bringing persistence and intensity. You filter distractions and prioritize what truly matters.

Example: Henrik cleared a full day to finalize the report, delivering ahead of deadline and without needing reminders.

In the workplace

You're known for discipline. You set clear goals, follow through, and expect others to do the same.

Watch out for

You may become narrow or impatient with changing priorities.

Example: You resisted adding a new client request because it "wasn't in the original plan", even though it was a smart strategic shift.

Coaching tip

Ask yourself: Where is my focus serving, and where might I need to zoom out?

19. TARGETED

What it can do

You pursue clear outcomes. You focus your energy where it creates results and avoid wasting time on what doesn't move the needle. You bring goal clarity and directness.

Example: During a busy quarter, Louise proposed skipping two meetings and focusing on two KPIs instead—freeing up time and improving delivery.

In the workplace

You drive momentum. You keep projects sharp and help teams stay aligned with measurable objectives.

Watch out for

You may lose patience with complexity or undervalue collaboration and process.

Example: You bypassed a team check-in to "just get it done," but missed important context that affected the outcome.

Coaching tip

Ask yourself: What's the shortest path, without cutting the wrong corners?

20. INITIATING

What it can do

You take action quickly. You rarely wait for direction, you prefer to start, test, and adjust. You energize teams by moving ideas into motion.

Example: When a potential partnership came up, Mark drafted a proposal and reached out, before the idea got stuck in endless planning.

In the workplace

You bring drive and proactivity. You reduce delay and are often the reason something got started at all.

Watch out for

You may start too many things or move without alignment.

Example: You kicked off a new pilot without informing key stakeholders, creating confusion and duplicated effort.

Coaching tip

Ask yourself: What needs to happen first, and who needs to come with me?

21. CONFIDENT

What it can do

You trust your judgment. You bring calm under pressure, stay grounded in your abilities, and take responsibility even when the outcome is uncertain.

Example: Asked to present with short notice, Anja said yes without hesitation, and delivered with clarity and presence.

In the workplace

You model self-assurance. You help others feel secure by showing that you can handle what comes your way.

Watch out for

You may overlook feedback or seem closed to input.

Example: You dismissed concerns about your proposal because you "knew it would work", missing insights that could have improved it.

Coaching tip

Ask yourself: What strength am I standing in, and where can I stay open, too?

22. VALUE-DRIVEN

What it can do

You lead with principles. You care deeply about meaning, ethics, and purpose, and help others stay aligned with what truly matters. You bring integrity into decisions, especially in moments of pressure.

Example: During a budget cut, Camilla argued to protect training funds, highlighting the long-term impact on employee development and culture.

In the workplace

You're the conscience of the team. You help navigate trade-offs with a values lens and ensure actions match intentions.

Watch out for

You may resist compromise or move slowly if something doesn't feel 100% aligned.

Example: You delayed approving a vendor because they didn't fully reflect company values, even though they were the best operational fit.

Coaching tip

Ask yourself: Where is alignment essential, and where is good enough, enough?

THE 6 INFLUENCING TALENTS

23. CHARMING

What it can do

You connect with ease. You disarm tension, build rapport quickly, and help others feel welcome. You bring warmth and approachability into every room.

Example: At a tense client meeting, Mads cracked a relevant joke, shifted the mood, and created a space where progress could happen.

In the workplace

You foster connection. You make it easier for others to engage, speak up, and relax—especially in high-stakes environments.

Watch out for

You may smooth things over instead of going deep, or avoid conflict to maintain good vibes.

Example: You supported everyone's opinion in a meeting—leaving the group with no real decision.

Coaching tip

Ask yourself: What truth needs to be said, beneath the charm?

24. IMPROVER

What it can do

You constantly raise the bar. You notice flaws, refine details, and push processes or products to be better. You bring energy for growth and progress.

Example: Line redesigned the onboarding flow, not because it was broken, but because it could be more intuitive and engaging.

In the workplace

You're a quality booster. You bring attention to what could be smoother, stronger, or smarter.

Watch out for

You may struggle to rest or let things stand as "good enough."

Example: You kept editing the deck, even after the deadline, frustrating teammates who needed to move on.

Coaching tip

Ask yourself: What already works, and where is improvement truly needed now?

25. COMPETITIVE

What it can do

You like to win. You measure progress, set benchmarks, and bring performance energy into teams. You're motivated by achievement, and help others level up.

Example: Jesper set a clear team goal and created a leaderboard—sparking friendly competition and record-breaking results.

In the workplace

You bring urgency and ambition. You help teams aim higher and take pride in what they achieve.

Watch out for

You may create pressure or forget collaboration if you focus too much on performance.

Example: You pushed your idea hard in a group setting, without fully hearing the team's concerns.

Coaching tip

Ask yourself: Where does healthy competition serve, and where does the team need unity instead?

26. OPTIMISTIC

What it can do

You uplift others. You naturally see possibilities, focus on what's working, and bring energy into conversations and projects. Optimism helps maintain momentum, even during uncertainty.

Example: When the team faced a series of rejections, Anne reminded them of past successes, reframed the challenges, and helped the group refocus on what was still possible.

In the workplace

You create a positive atmosphere. People feel more confident and resilient around you. You help shift focus from problems to solutions.

Watch out for

You may overlook risks or ignore early signs of trouble. Others might feel unheard if you move too quickly to the bright side.

Example: If you reassure the team everything would work out without acknowledging their valid concerns, which can make some feel dismissed.

Coaching tip

Ask yourself: What's the most constructive way to hold both optimism and realism in this situation?

27. CONTROLLING

What it can do

You take charge. You're comfortable leading, setting direction, and making firm decisions. You often step up when others hesitate.

Example: When a project lost momentum, Morten restructured the roles, redefined timelines, and reactivated the group.

In the workplace

You lead with clarity. You provide certainty, take responsibility, and offer direction during confusion.

Watch out for

You may over-direct or reduce autonomy in others.

Example: You assigned detailed tasks to your team instead of letting them plan—leaving them feeling disempowered.

Coaching tip

Ask yourself: What part of control creates progress, and what part could be safely shared?

28. DEVELOPER

What it can do

You grow people. You spot potential, give feedback constructively, and enjoy supporting others' learning and evolution. You bring a coaching mindset into everyday leadership.

Example: When a colleague struggled with presenting, Emil offered targeted encouragement and practical tips—boosting both skill and confidence.

In the workplace

You create learning environments. You care not just about results, but how people grow while getting there.

Watch out for

You may over-invest in others who aren't ready, or neglect your own growth.

Example: You continued mentoring a resistant teammate for months, while your own priorities fell behind.

Coaching tip

Ask yourself: Where is the energy for growth mutual, and where might I need to shift focus?

THE 6
RELATING TALENTS

29. EMPATHIC

What it can do
You sense emotions intuitively. You understand people's inner state, often before they speak. You create psychological safety and make others feel seen and supported.

Example: After a difficult me eting, Sofie privately checked in with a teammate she sensed was hurt. Helping them feel respected and re-engaged.

In the workplace
You create emotional clarity. You notice how others are doing and bring compassion into decision-making.

Watch out for

You may absorb others' emotions too much, or avoid tension to protect feelings.

Example: You didn't raise a performance concern because you didn't want to upset the person, even though the issue affected the whole team.

Coaching tip

Ask yourself: What does care look like in action, not just emotion?

30. INCLUSIVE

What it can do

You bring people in. You notice who's left out, invite broader perspectives, and create space for voices that may otherwise be unheard.

Example: During a leadership roundtable, Andreas paused to ask the two quietest members for their input—unlocking insights the group would've missed.

In the workplace

You foster belonging. You're attentive to group dynamics and make collaboration more democratic.

Watch out for

You may over-consult or slow decisions in the name of inclusion.

> Example: You postponed a plan multiple times to gather input from everyone—losing valuable time.

Coaching tip

Ask yourself: Who truly needs to be involved—and where can I lead with what's already known?

31. INDIVIDUALIZING

What it can do

You see what makes people unique. You tailor support, communication, and expectations based on each person's strengths and needs. This helps others feel recognized and empowered.

Example: Managing her team, Maria gave each direct report a slightly different development plan, based on their learning style and role ambitions.

In the workplace

You personalize. You don't treat people the same, you treat them fairly, according to who they are.

Watch out for

You may over-customize or avoid setting common expectations.

Example: You made so many exceptions for individuals that the team lost its sense of cohesion.

Coaching tip

Ask yourself: Where do people need individual space, and where do they need shared direction?

32. COMMUNICATING

What it can do

You express ideas clearly. Whether through writing, speaking, or visuals, you make complex things simple and help people understand and connect.

Example: Emma rewrote a technical update into a short, visual memo—making it accessible and useful across departments.

In the workplace

You bring clarity. You help teams align, stakeholders engage, and messages land with impact.

Watch out for

You may talk more than you listen, or over-focus on presentation over substance.

Example: You delivered a great pitch, but missed two key objections because you didn't pause for questions.

Coaching tip

Ask yourself: What's the message, and what do they truly need to hear now?

33. CONNECTING

What it can do

You build relationships naturally. You're energized by social interaction and enjoy creating networks across silos, levels, or backgrounds.

Example: During a global project, Louise linked people from three departments who didn't usually collaborate, accelerating problem-solving.

In the workplace

You're a connector. You spot who should talk to whom, and help them do it.

Watch out for

You may prioritize relationships over tasks or find it hard to say no.

> Example: You agreed to three cross-functional projects because you liked the people—spreading yourself too thin.

Coaching tip

Ask yourself: Where does this connection serve the goal, and where might I need to protect my energy?

34. MEDIATING

What it can do

You help resolve tension. You listen well, stay neutral, and guide others through conflict with calm and fairness. People trust you when emotions run high.

Example: When two colleagues clashed, Kasper facilitated a short meeting that got them back on track, without taking sides.

In the workplace

You build bridges. You see both sides and help groups move from disagreement to understanding.

Watch out for

You may avoid choosing sides, even when leadership requires it.

Example: You stayed "in the middle" too long in a value conflict, leaving others confused about your position.

Coaching tip

Ask yourself: When do I need to help reconcile, and when do I need to take a stand?

The previous points covered the 34 talents visible in your talent graph in the test.

Just below the talent graph the four archetypes are shown. Therefore, we'll now dive into these.

THE FOUR ARCHETYPES

Every TT38 talent falls into one or more out of four archetypes: Thinking (blue), Relating (green), Influencing (red) and/or Striving (purple). These describe the type of energy your top talents express, what drives your attention, your contribution, and your behavior in work life.

The description below shows how your talents are distributed across those four areas. It helps you understand the bigger pattern: Do you primarily collaborate and lead with ideas and knowledge, with people connection, with action, or with influence?

Below is a breakdown of each archetype. With examples of how it may show up in your individual work, and what it could mean for team dynamics.

1. THE THINKING TALENTS

Talents in this archetype are about analyzing, synthesizing, understanding systems, and seeing patterns. You likely enjoy deep thinking, reflective space, and complex problem-solving.

Talents in this archetype

Analyzing, Assessing, Co-ordinating, Contextual, Holistic, Innovative, Inquiring, Just, Reflective, Researching, Strategic, Visionary.

Individual example: Someone with strong Strategic and Analyzing talents might be known for making smart long-term decisions based on both logic and foresight.

Team implication
Thinking talents offer insight and pattern recognition. But if a team has too much thinking talents and little striving or relating talents, it may get stuck in planning without execution.

2. THE RELATING TALENTS
These talents focus on people, emotions, inclusion, and human-based collaboration. You're likely attuned to others' moods and needs and motivated by belonging and meaningful relationships.

Talents in this archetype
Communicating, Connecting, Empathic, Inclusive, Individualizing, Mediating.

Individual example: Someone with Empathic and Mediating talents may act as the emotional anchor in a team, helping resolve conflicts and keep morale high.

Team implication
Relating talents build trust, cohesion, and psychological safety. A team with a lot of relating talents often feels supportive, but if not supported with striving talents the team may avoid difficult conversations or struggle with pace.

3. THE INFLUENCING TALENTS
Influencing talents shape how you affect others' thinking, behavior, or perception. These talents bring energy, communication, persuasion, and clarity when leading.

Talents in this archetype

Charming, Competitive, Controlling, Developer, Improver, Optimistic.

Individual example: Someone with Optimistic and Charming talents may be a natural spokesperson or pitch leader-engaging and motivating.

Team implication

Influencing talents help mobilize teams, sell ideas, and gain buy-in. But if a team leans too heavily here, it may overpromise or under-deliver, without grounding in details or process (unless the other archetypes are well represented too).

4. THE STRIVING TALENTS

These talents are about drive, focus, structure, and execution. People with a majority of striving talents tend to be goal-oriented, organized, and motivated by results or progress.

Talents in this archetype
Confident, Flexible, Focused, Initiating, Orderly, Prominent, Responsible, Targeted, Trouble-shooter, Value-driven.

Individual example: A person with Responsible and Orderly talents may be the one who brings deadlines to life, ensures consistency, and keeps everything on track.

Team implication
Striving talents push for outcomes and hold people accountable. Teams high in this dimension get things done, but may forget to pause, reflect, or care for the human experience.

What to watch for

Everyone has a unique combination of these four. Some people are deeply specialized in one area; others are more evenly balanced.

- A lack of Thinking talents might mean less long-term vision or critical evaluation.
- A lack of Relating might cause blind spots in team wellbeing.
- A lack of Influencing could lead to ideas being ignored, no matter how good they are.
- A lack of Striving may result in creative stagnation or weak execution.

The insight isn't about fixing a gap—it's about knowing it and finding others who complement you.

The test and your talent graph guide you to discover four hidden notes. Therefore, these four hidden talents is the next thing that we'll explore.

THE FOUR HIDDEN TALENTS

These talents, as we call the hidden talents, are indicators on how your operating system works. Some of them are a bit more complex to figure out, yet very important for how you play your sound.

Those are:
- Your pace of processing or decision making
- How you project
- Your IQ indicator
- Your EQ

THE FAST PACED OR THE THOROUGH THINKER

The statistics of the test show if you process things fast or needs more time to think things through. This of course has a huge impact on your work life and collaborations. If you're aware of this, it can be used as one of your strongest assets.

What it can do

If you have completed the test in less than 34 minutes, you are faster than average. This indicates that you are faster than others to get to the bottom of things and to reach solutions. On the other hand, if you used more than 34 minutes to respond, the test indicates that you embrace thorough thinking and need more time before making a discission.

In the workplace
Having a fast-paced brain typically means that you can see patterns and jump to conclusions very quickly. You can handle many things on your plate because you see things clearer faster. On the contrary, being a thorough thinker, you need more time to handle tasks, and you like to make sure that you have thought things through before jumping to conclusions or solutions.

Watch out for
When having a fast-paced brain there is a risk of you being impatient. Being unaware can cause you running people over or losing them either by start or maybe halfway. Being a thorough thinker can slow down discission making or processes.

Coaching tip

Ask yourself: In what situations is this a strong asset and in what situations does this become a pitfall?

HOW YOU PROJECT

Maybe you have noticed that some people "own the room" or "take their space" more than others? This is what this part is all about. Some people have a strong presence, some people don't make any fuss out of themselves, or some people can differentiate from situation to situation.

PLAYING EVERY NOTE LOUDLY

In the statistics of your test under *respond distribution*, you can see how explicit your talents are expressed. If the curve is like a smile, it means that your talents are very visible to others. You take up your space and everyone notice your presence in the room.

What it can do
People know you and quickly get who you are. Your visible way of approaching life is great when you need to spread your vision, thoughts and ideas. You like to be seen and heard and have a strong potential of being a great speaker.

Watch out for
Being extroverted and tending to speak a lot can lead to fatigue in others. Because you might have a hard time giving others their space or blending in with the crowd. This can cause people to feel overheard or not seen. There is also a risk of missing out on important views and perspectives.

Coaching tip

Ask yourself: When could it benefit processes to listen more?

PLAYING EVERY NOTE VERY STILL

If the curve is a reversed smile, a sad mouth, it indicates that you play out your talents more subtle, and you don't make any fuzz out of yourself. Maybe you have a harder time taking up your space in the room – giving it away to others.

What it can do

You're not comfortable with attention and like giving the space to others. Maybe you give your thoughts and speak your mind in a subtle way or even through others. Blending in with e.g., a team is a great skill because the collective knowledge will easier be prone coming into play.

Watch out for

You can be seen as invisible to others. This can lead to you being not heard nor seen. The great views you have on e.g., tasks, solutions etc. are at risk to be overheard. Further, your boundaries to be crossed are at risk.

Coaching tip

Ask yourself: In what situations could I or the team benefit from me speaking up my mind? And how could I do it?

PLAYING WITH NUANCES

When your talent curve is gently curved, like a wave or a phrase in music, it suggests you have the ability to let your talents flow with nuance. You don't always play at full volume, nor do you mute yourself completely. You sense when to step forward and when to create space.

What it can do

You're able to shift gears with grace. In one moment, you may lead with confidence; in the next, you let others shine. This balance allows you to co-create, adjust to the energy in the room, and bring harmony to dynamic environments.

Example: In a cross-functional meeting, you lead a section with clarity, then step back to actively listen and lift others' contributions—keeping momentum without dominating.

Watch out for

Your ability to adapt is powerful—but if unspoken, it can be misunderstood. Others may not always grasp why you pause, shift, or slow down. If you adjust silently, it might come off as indecisiveness or even control.

Example: In a team setting, you step back to avoid crowding a colleague's idea—but your silence is read as disengagement.

Coaching tip
Ask yourself: Am I tuning in—and also letting others know what I'm hearing?

Your intuitive pacing is a gift. Just don't forget to bring others along in your rhythm.

POSSIBILITY OF HAVING A HIGH IQ

Please read the headline of this paragraph again. The headline is thoughtful chosen. The test alone cannot specify your IQ, but it can give you a strong sense of it. There are some parameters that all need to be fulfilled before the guess takes shape. The test indicates a probability of 70-84 percent that you possess a high IQ if:

1. You have twelve or more top talents.
2. Among your top talents, you have a high score of thinking talents—three or even more give higher chances
3. You finished the test quickly (between 18 – 28 minutes).
4. You had few contradictions, under 15 percent in the field of control questions.

What it can do

If you could check all the above boxes then we recommend having your IQ tested. Having a high IQ means that your brain has higher levels of capabilities in the use of the top talents. You can process, think and see patterns very fast. Things that others either never would have thought of or would have used much more time to outthink than you.

Watch out for

Your brain runs fast and might solve complex issues with ease and see patterns and ways of doings that others maybe even cannot follow. This is a gift but, sometimes you can disconnect with others or even lose them on the way. Your train has left the station several days ago but the one you collaborate with is not onboard, they are still at the station.

Coaching tip

Ask yourself: In what situations do I need to pause and reassure I'm connected to the people I collaborate with?

HIGH EQ – THE EMOTIONALLY INTELLIGENT

The test can show if you have a high EQ, but also if it's hard or soft. People with a high EQ have relating or influencing talents and/or the strategic/holistic at the top. The difference between the soft and the hard EQ profile is that the hard EQ is more a strategic emotional intelligence rather than the "real thing." Having a hard EQ isn't necessarily harmful but used with awareness can be an advantage in sales or as a leader. These are the characteristics that point to a high EQ.

Soft EQ profile is validated if one or more of the talents in each of the different aspects are present in the top talents:

- *The social aspect*: Connecting, Inclusive, Communicating, Optimistic, Charming.
- *The understanding aspect:* Mediating, Holistic, Developer, Connecting, Individualizing

- *Reading people*: Empathic, Individualizing, Holistic (Mediating, Developer)

The Hard IQ profile is validated if one or more talents of the following aspects are present:

Influencing people: Strategic, Charming, Communicating, Developer, Optimistic, Initiating (Improver + optimistic).

What it can do

People with a high soft EQ are capable of influencing and relating to others in the most appropriate way. If your EQ is both soft and hard you actually have a coach potential. We both (Josefine and Gitte) have this unique combination.

Watch out for

High EQ can create challenges in having an oversensitivity towards others' needs and behavior. You can either accept too much or even undermine yourself. If you have a lower EQ with little or no relating or influencing talents as the top talents nor the strategic or holistic as one of the top 3 you can be prone to mistaken others' intentions or behavior.

Coaching tip

Ask yourself: When is it that I let others' needs and behavior into my system eating up my energy? And when being aware what can I do to get back to myself?

You can use your knowledge of the 34 visible and the 4 hidden talents as a way to inform how you choose to contribute—either mute your natural strengths or let them resonate. Use it to notice where your energy is met with the right kind of challenge. The sound of your talent chord will guide you, if you let it.

Let it lead you toward work that sounds like you using your talent combinations or chords.

UNDERSTANDING TALENT COMBINATIONS, OR CHORDS

Your TT38 profile shows more than just individual talents, it reveals a unique Talent Chord.

Just like musical notes blend to create a chord, your talents combine to shape how you think, make decisions, and lead. One person's chord may be energetic and fast-moving. Another person's may be grounding, steady, and intuitive. There's no right or wrong. Only different ways of resonating with the world.

UNDERSTANDING YOUR TALENT CHORD HELPS YOU

- Make sense of why you lead the way you do
- Recognize your natural impact on others
- Adapt and grow without losing yourself.

In the following pages, you'll find examples of named Talent Chords—combinations we often see in leaders. They're not labels, but mirrors. Use them to reflect: Which ones feel close to my own? When does my chord play well, and when does it go off-key?

As all the talents, the chords also have

advantages and disadvantages, when unbalanced or overused.

It reveals not just individual talents, but how talents interact—either reinforcing or contradicting each other. This is where deeper insight and real personal development take off.

WHY CHORDS MATTER

Talents don't work in isolation. In real life, they act together, sometimes creating synergy, sometimes causing internal tension. The definition is this:

- Strengthening Combinations: Talents that amplify each other in the same direction.
- Contradictory Combinations: Talents that pull in opposite directions, creating dynamic tension.

UNDERSTANDING BOTH TYPES HELPS PEOPLE

- Leverage their strongest patterns
- Balance potentially rigid or extreme tendencies
- Know which combinations to be aware off or use to outcome in the best possible way.

CONTRADICTORY COMBINATIONS

These create paradoxes—but that's not bad. They often reflect deep potential or creative tension. You might have both Orderly and Flexible. Which one ranks higher? Are they both in the top talent 3 of your top talents, or is one just above the mid-range line? Their placement determines how they play out.

For example,

- Orderly (score: 10.3) and Flexible (score: 6.6) → You'll default to structure, but adaptability is accessible with effort.
- Both score high → You are both structured and adaptable—rare and valuable in agile teams, for example.

Chord	Description
Connecting + Competitive	A "Friendly Challenger" – great in client-facing roles, mixes warmth with ambition.
Flexible + Orderly	An "Adaptable Organizer" – combines structure with openness. Rare and useful in changing environments.

Chord	Description
Innovative + Assessing	A "Refined Creator" – generates ideas and tests them critically. Strong in product roles.
Reflective + Initiating	"Fast & Thoughtful" – balances careful thinking with decisive action. Great in strategy roles.
Contextual + Visionary	"Past Meets Future" – sees long-term patterns and emerging trends. A strategic compass.
Controlling + Empathic	"Directive with Care" – leads with clarity while staying attuned to others. A balanced people manager.

Be mindful that a strong talent may need a contradictory one to balance it—or someone else on the team to bring it into play.

THE HOW-HARD-CAN-IT-BE PROFILE

Talents: Focused + Responsible + Co-ordinating + Trouble-shooter

Quality:

This chord thrives in execution. People with this combination cut through complexity and get things done—fast. They are structured, accountable, and relentless in solving problems. They don't dwell on the "why not", they move straight to the "how."

They shine in environments that need operational rigor, momentum, and own-ership. In crisis or chaos, they become the reliable engine behind the scenes.

Example: During a tight production window, someone with this chord sees that the team is overcomplicating logistics. They create a clear plan, reassign tasks, fix bottlenecks, and keep the project moving.

Watch out for

This profile can become impatient with delays, ambiguity, or people who "overthink." They may push too hard for action, skipping over reflection, emotion, or broader strategy. At worst, their sense of control and urgency can overwhelm others.

Example: In a team meeting, they dismiss a colleague's big-picture concern as "not relevant right now." While they meant to maintain momentum, the effect was silencing and deflating.

Coaching Tip

Ask yourself: Am I solving the right problem, or just the next one?

And: Who needs to come along, not just be directed?

There are millions of talent combinations. That is one of the reasons why we like this tool. Not two people are the same and looking at the combinations in each profile makes it clear how each individual has its own unique tune. But nevertheless, there are talent chords that we see again and again. You might recognize some of these.

In appendix 1, you can dive into more examples the strengthening chords, such the perfectionist, the steady climber, and the adaptive architect.

Now you're ready to explore the dimensions of the report by yourself. If you belong to a team, that's where a team test could come in.

THE POWER OF A SHARED SOUND

TEAM TESTING MATTERS

Even though people praise some leaders as if they were saints. Superman doesn't exist. Not one person is perfect. Nobody has all talents. But a team with talents that complement each other can be outstanding and much better together than each individual on their own.

Knowing your own talent chord is powerful. But something special happens when an entire team tunes in together. A team test reveals not just individual strengths, it reveals the collective pattern. It gives the team a shared language, clearer dynamics, and a way to build not just performance, but trust.

WHAT IT IS AND HOW IT WORKS

A TT38 team profile is built by combining the individual talent profiles of everyone in the team. The result is a visual and narrative overview of how the team is composed:

- Which talents are dominant
- Where there are blind spots or gaps
- What drivers are shared (or not)
- How team roles are distributed
- Where friction might occur, and why.

It becomes a mirror for the team, showing what might have been felt but never clearly seen. And with that clarity, new conversations become possible.

For the individual, a team test deepens awareness of how your strengths land in a group. It also shows what others bring that you might overlook or take for granted.

It helps you:
- Understand how your style affects others
- Appreciate the value of very different talent chords
- Know when to lead, and when to step back

For the team, the value is exponential:
- More trust and psychological safety
- Clearer collaboration, because expectations are aligned
- Less wasted energy on miscommunication
- A shared vocabulary for feedback and growth
- Better meetings, smarter division of tasks, and more respect for difference

It shifts the focus from who's right to what's needed, and who's naturally best suited to offer it.

WHAT IT REQUIRES

Like any instrument, the tool only works if it's used. A team test brings insight, but insight only turns into value when there's openness, curiosity, and a willingness to grow.

The result isn't just better teamwork. It can be a work culture where people feel seen, understood, and are set up to succeed—together.

And that's when the team becomes more than the sum of its parts.

It becomes a sound of its own.

REFLECTION

If your team were a piece of music;

What part would you naturally play?

What might you be missing—or overlooking?

And what would change if you all played with full awareness of each other's sound?

Take a moment.

What insight do you want to bring back to your team?

COACH YOURSELF – TAKE SMALL STEPS

We have a mantra.

"Even small changes in behavior can have a huge impact."

Often, it's the small steps that will create the change. Like a small stone thrown in a still lake causes the spread of rings. It's also the smaller steps that are easier to do and overcome. In our coaching practice we use this approach:

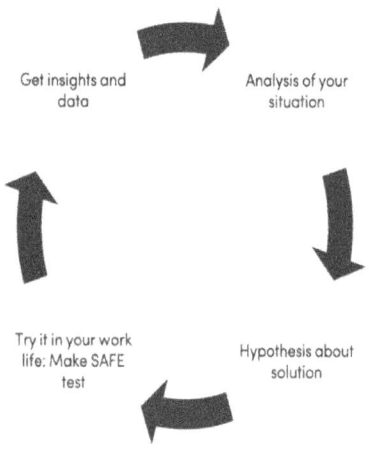

Figure 1: The SAFE-test method©, Josefine Campbell, 2022

This SAFE-test Method is a practical coaching approach we use to help you turn your TT38 talent insights into action. It supports you in developing new behaviors that stick—through testing, reflection, and iteration. You can use it this way:

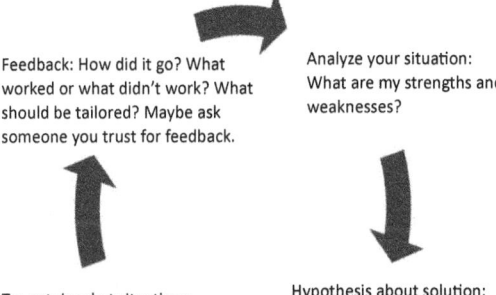

Figure 2: The SAFE-test method explained

As you can see this approach is a circle that will never end. It can be used in every aspect of life, wherever you need a change.

CLOSING THE PHRASE— NOT THE SONG

We don't always choose when the tempo shifts.

Sometimes change comes fast.

Other times, it asks us to wait, to listen, to realign.

This guide isn't meant to give you all the answers. It's here to help you ask better questions, about what you're naturally made for, and how you want to shape your time, your leadership, and your life.

As you move through moments of

choice, big or small, we hope you'll return to your talent chords.

Use them to guide decisions.

To recover your energy.

To find direction when things feel noisy.

And to remember; you don't need to play every note. Just the ones that are truly yours.

Stay close to your sound. And let it lead.

Kind regards,
GITTE & JOSEFINE

P.S. Please feel free to add us on LinkedIn or get in contact if you have any questions.

APPENDIX 1: EXAMPLES OF STRENGTHENING CHORDS

THE VISION ANCHOR

Talent chord: Visionary, Holistic, Value-Driven

Quality

You lead with meaning. You naturally see what could be, and ensure it connects to a bigger purpose. You bring depth and direction, helping teams see not just where they're going, but why.

Example: In a change project, you refocus the team by reminding them how this ties into long-term strategy and shared values, restoring clarity and motivation.

Watch out for

You may hesitate to act without full alignment. Colleagues under pressure might feel your pace is too slow or too philosophical.

Example: You delay launching a campaign because one element doesn't fully reflect the company's values, even though the team is ready.

Coaching tip

Ask yourself: What's "aligned enough" to move forward? Can I act now and refine as we go?

THE PERFECTIONIST

Talent chord: Detail-Oriented, Analyzing, Responsible

Quality

You hold a high bar. You spot flaws others miss, think deeply, and take full ownership of results. You're the one who polishes, corrects, and finishes strong.

Example: You identify an unnoticed error in a board report—saving your leader from presenting wrong data.

Watch out for

You might overwork tasks or over-identify with the outcome. Perfection can cost time, trust, or collaboration.

Example: You spend hours improving a document no one asked you to refine, and miss a chance to involve others.

Coaching tip

Ask yourself: What matters more here: control or contribution?

THE PERFECTIONIST V2

Talent chord: Improver, Orderly, Responsible (+ Assessing)

Quality

You take pride in excellence. You're driven to improve everything you touch, create order from chaos, and take full ownership for delivering the best possible outcome. You combine structure with sharp judgment, making you a trusted guardian of quality.

Example: When reviewing a policy draft, you not only spot inconsistencies but reorganize the layout and wording so it flows better and matches company values.

Watch out for

You may get stuck in endless refining or expect others to match your standards without realizing it. Over-control or criticism (even internal) can stall collaboration.

Example: You delay launching a team project because you're still adjusting the process documents, even though the team is already ready to go.

Coaching tip

Ask yourself: What's good enough for now? Can I deliver value, even if it's not perfect yet?

THE EMPATHIC STABILIZER

Talent chord: Empathic, Connecting, Holistic

Quality

You sense people and dynamics. You notice what's not said, read emotional undercurrents, and help restore calm. In team life, you're the one other quietly rely on to keep harmony and belonging.

Example: In a tense meeting, you acknowledge a colleague's stress and shift the tone of the room—without being asked.

Watch out for

You may absorb too much emotion or avoid conflict to keep peace. Others might see you as soft, even when you have strong insights.

Example: You don't challenge a poor idea because the person behind it seems fragile, even if the team needs you to speak up.

Coaching tip

Ask yourself: What truth needs to be spoken with care?

THE FIRESTARTER
Talent chord: Initiating, Confident, Competitive

Quality
You move first. You're bold, decisive, and thrive under pressure. You bring spark, energy, and visible action. In teams, you're often the one pushing forward while others hesitate.

Example: You pitch a bold client solution before the competition even replies, creating momentum and opportunity.

Watch out for

Speed can turn into dominance. You may move ahead without consensus or skip listening when it matters.

Example: You set a new direction during a meeting, without checking if the team was aligned or ready.

Coaching tip

Ask yourself: Where could I hold back briefly to bring others with me?

THE QUIET STRATEGIST

Talent chord: Reflective, Strategic, Individualizing

Quality

You think before you act, and when you speak, it matters. You see patterns, think long-term, and adapt your approach to each person. You lead through insight, not noise.

Example: You reframe a team issue in one sentence that shifts the group's direction, without dominating the discussion.

Watch out for

You may stay too internal or hesitate to act when others need clarity. People might not hear your perspective unless invited.

Example: You've solved a challenge in your head, but didn't share it, and the team kept struggling.

Coaching tip

Ask yourself: What value am I holding back that could serve the group now?

THE BOLD IMPROVER

Talent chord: Improver, Innovative, Optimistic

Quality

You see how things could be better, and believe it's possible. You combine creativity with positivity, challenging the status quo in a way that lifts others up. Change feels energizing to you, not threatening.

Example: In a team process review, you suggest a faster, better way of working—sparking buy-in by painting a hopeful picture of the outcome.

Watch out for

Your ideas may overwhelm others or come too fast. You may underestimate resistance to change or forget to bring people along.

Example: You present a fully baked new system, without checking whether the team felt the old one was broken.

Coaching tip

Ask yourself: Who needs to help shape this improvement, so they'll own it, too?

THE PURPOSE-DRIVEN LEADER
Talent chord: Value-Driven, Responsible, Strategic

Quality
You lead from inner conviction. You align actions to values and connect daily decisions to long-term purpose. You bring trust, clarity, and consistency—especially in uncertain moments.

Example: When asked to cut corners on a proposal, you respectfully decline, and help craft a solution that's both ethical and effective.

Watch out for

You may be rigid when compromise is needed. Others might experience you as "principled to a fault."

Example: You reject a project collaboration that doesn't fully reflect your values, without exploring ways to shape it from within.

Coaching tip

Ask yourself: Where can I live my values without needing perfect alignment?

THE RELATIONAL GLUE

Talent chord: Connecting, Inclusive, Mediating

Quality

You create belonging. You naturally bridge people, invite diverse voices, and hold space for multiple perspectives. In teams, you're often the one who sees who's not being heard and makes sure they are.

Example: During a heated discussion, you step in, not to take sides, but to help everyone feel seen and move forward together.

Watch out for

You might avoid tension or suppress your own voice to keep peace. People-pleasing can dilute your impact.

Example: You say yes to everyone's ideas, even when you know they conflict, because you don't want to disappoint anyone.

Coaching tip

Ask yourself: How can I hold the group together and speak with clarity?

THE CHALLENGER

Talent chord: Just, Competitive, Prominent

Quality

You stand for fairness, and you want to win. You challenge inefficiency, hold others to high standards, and aren't afraid to speak up. You give voice to what others think but don't say.

Example: In a leadership team meeting, you challenge unequal promotion decisions and advocate for a more transparent process.

Watch out for

Your drive may come across as confrontational or harsh if not balanced with empathy.

Example: You shut down a colleague's idea too abruptly, thereby missing a chance to build it into something stronger together.

Coaching tip

Ask yourself: How can I lead the challenge with strength and respect?

THE CALM RESPONDER
Talent chord: Reflective, Flexible, Empathic

Quality

You bring calm, presence, and perspective. You don't rush to react. Instead, you observe, listen, and choose your response. In tense or uncertain situations, others feel grounded by you.

Example: When a project crisis hits, you slow the conversation, ask thoughtful questions, and help the group settle before acting.

Watch out for
You may stay too silent, waiting for more clarity, while others need a visible lead.

Example: Your team interprets your calm as disengagement. When in fact, you're simply taking time to reflect.

Coaching tip
Ask yourself: *What quiet leadership does this moment need, and when do I need to raise my voice?*

THE INCLUSIVE LEADER

Talent chord: Inclusive, Individualizing, Communicating

Quality

You create space for everyone to contribute. You notice what makes people unique and give them room to shine. You explain things clearly, adapt your message to each person, and ensure people feel valued.

Example: During a strategy session, you draw out a quiet team member's insight, then translate it in a way that the full group connects with.

Watch out for

You may over-accommodate or water down strong messages to avoid discomfort.

Example: You rewrite a message three times trying to make it work for everyone—losing impact and momentum.

Coaching tip

Ask yourself: Where can clarity serve the group better than comfort?

THE DRIVEN STARTER

Talent chord: Initiating, Focused, Optimistic

Quality

You get things moving. Fast. You're naturally positive, decisive, and drawn to clear objectives. You love turning a vision into momentum. Others often say, "Nothing would have happened without you."

Example: You rally the team to begin a stalled project by breaking it into manageable steps and generating energy.

Watch out for

You may rush ahead without reflection or full alignment. Some may feel pushed or left behind.

Example: You finalize a plan before all voices have been heard, missing early feedback that could prevent problems later.

Coaching tip

Ask yourself: What's urgent, and what needs one more perspective first?

THE LOYAL OPERATOR

Talent chord: Orderly, Responsible, Contextual

Quality

You provide structure, consistency, and reliability. You remember what worked before, keep processes running smoothly, and take ownership for outcomes. People know they can count on you.

Example: You maintain critical workflows during times of chaos, ensuring stability for your team and stakeholders.

Watch out for

You may resist change that threatens order or traditions. Others might find you inflexible in new situations.

Example: You dismiss a new tech tool too quickly because "the old one works fine"—missing a real opportunity for improvement.

Coaching tip

Ask yourself: What stability do I want to protect, and where might I need to stretch?

THE AMBITIOUS INFLUENCER

Talent chord: Prominent, Competitive, Charming

Quality

You love to stand out, and lift others up as you do. You bring presence, drive, and confidence to the room. Your ambition is inspiring, and your ability to connect makes others want to follow.

Example: In a pitch, you speak with passion and confidence, winning trust not just with facts, but with presence.

Watch out for
You may unintentionally overshadow others or focus too much on personal wins.

Example: You take the spotlight in a joint presentation—leaving your quieter co-presenter in the background.

Coaching tip
Ask yourself: What part of this success is mine to share, and who else can I help shine?

THE SOLUTION SEEKER

Talent chord: Trouble-Shooter, Strategic, Developer

Quality

You solve problems and develop people. You naturally see paths forward and believe that even tough challenges can lead to growth. You don't just fix, you build.

Example: When a project fails, you turn the post-mortem into a coaching moment and help the team create a stronger next version.

Watch out for

You may jump too quickly to solutions without sitting with discomfort or fully exploring the root issue.

Example: You redirect a team's frustra-tion before they've fully voiced it, causing unresolved tensions to linger.

Coaching tip

Ask yourself: What does this situation need first: resolution or reflection?

THE STRATEGIC DRIVER
Talent chord: Strategic, Focused, Targeted

Quality

You know where you're going—and how to get there. You think ahead, cut through distractions, and channel energy toward goals. You drive progress with precision and purpose.

Example: You guide a team through ambiguity by laying out clear priorities and milestones, helping everyone stay aligned and motivated.

Watch out for

You may become overly goal-fixated or dismiss input that slows you down.

Example: You reject a colleague's alternative approach because it doesn't match your initial strategy, even though it might offer value.

Coaching tip

Ask yourself: Where could opening to input sharpen (not slow) your strategy?

THE COURAGEOUS CORRECTOR
Talent chord: Just, Responsible, Communicating

Quality
You speak up when things feel off. You have a strong sense of fairness and clarity, and you're not afraid to challenge norms or raise your voice for what's right.

Example: When a colleague's idea is dismissed without cause, you step in respectfully and bring it back to the table.

Watch out for
You may become overly corrective or blunt if emotions run high.

Example: You speak truth to power, but your tone shuts down conversation instead of inviting it.

Coaching tip
Ask yourself: How can I lead correction with courage, and connection?

THE CREATIVE CHALLENGER

Talent chord: Innovative, Analyzing, Competitive

Quality

You break rules, for the right reasons. You generate new ideas, question assumptions, and push for excellence. You energize others by proving that things can always be better.

Example: You challenge an outdated product model and propose a bold redesign that unlocks a new market.

Watch out for

You may dismiss traditional or structured approaches too quickly.

Example: You reject a colleague's plan as "old thinking", even though parts of it could support your idea.

Coaching tip

Ask yourself: What tradition might still carry wisdom, and how can I shape it rather than scrap it?

THE RELIABLE PRODUCER
Talent chord: Orderly, Responsible, Developer

Quality

You create dependable results. You take pride in doing things right, helping others grow, and ensuring every detail is in place. You build solid, lasting foundations.

Example: You mentor a junior colleague through a complex report, making sure both the product and the person grow.

Watch out for

You may struggle with ambiguity or slow-down in messy, creative phases.

> Example: You spend time creating detailed processes in a pilot phase that needed experimentation, not perfection.

Coaching tip

Ask yourself: Where does consistency help, and where does flexibility serve more?

THE CONFIDENT MOVER

Talent chord: Confident, Initiating, Prominent

Quality

You act boldly. You move fast, trust your instincts, and lead from the front. Others follow you because you radiate certainty—even in uncertain situations.

Example: You step into a new role mid-project and quickly reframe priorities to move things forward.

Watch out for

You may overlook risks or move too fast for others to feel involved.

Example: You announce a change in direction without checking whether others have the context to follow.

Coaching tip

Ask yourself: What one pause could help others catch up, without slowing me down?

THE REFLECTIVE DEVELOPER

Talent chord: Reflective, Developer, Individualizing

Quality

You help people grow, quietly and intentionally. You listen deeply, observe patterns, and support others' development through thoughtful feedback and customized guidance.

Example: You help a team member build confidence by pointing out unnoticed strengths and offering targeted support.

Watch out for

You may hesitate to act or stay too internal in fast-paced settings.

Example: You notice someone is strug-gling but wait too long to offer help, missing the moment of impact.

Coaching tip

Ask yourself: What reflection needs to turn into a small action today?

THE CULTURAL ANCHOR
Talent chord: Value-Driven, Holistic, Mediating

Quality
You care about the way things are done. You bring people together around shared values, resolve tensions, and align culture with strategy. People feel safe and seen around you.

Example: You intervene during a conflict to help both sides see what's really at stake, bringing them back to common ground.

Watch out for

You may avoid difficult trade-offs or move slowly in moments that require fast decisions.

Example: You hesitate to approve a decision that feels misaligned, even though delay might cost the team progress.

Coaching tip

Ask yourself: How can I protect what matters without preventing what's needed?

THE ASSERTIVE ARCHITECT

Talent chord: Controlling, Co-ordinating, Strategic

Quality

You design how things work, and then make them work. You think long-term, create structure, and take charge of execution. You bring order to chaos.

Example: You build a clear plan for scaling a business unit and rally people around the structure with confidence.

Watch out for

You may over-control or limit others' creative input.

> Example: You assign tasks too rigidly, leaving team members disengaged or underused.

Coaching tip

Ask yourself: Where can I lead the process, and still leave room for shared ownership?

THE FUTURE GUIDE
Talent chord: Visionary, Inquiring, Developer

Quality

You're always evolving and help others do the same. You connect future possibilities with learning and growth. Others look to you for direction, inspiration, and insight.

Example: You spot a new market trend, explore it deeply, and guide your team into building future-ready skills.

Watch out for

You may become abstract or drift from the here-and-now.

Example: You research endlessly and lose touch with the team's immediate needs.

Coaching tip

Ask yourself: How can I connect tomorrow's ideas with today's action?

THE EMOTIONAL LISTENER

Talent chord: Empathic, Communicating, Reflective

Quality

You don't just hear; people you speak with feel heard. You notice nuance, communicate with sensitivity, and help others name what's going on. You often provide clarity just by being present.

Example: A teammate vents frustration. You listen, reframe their concern, and help them move forward with confidence.

Watch out for

You may carry emotional weight or forget to express your own needs.

> Example: You support others through stress, but don't let anyone support you.

Coaching tip

Ask yourself: What do I need to say out loud today—for me?

THE ADAPTIVE ARCHITECT

Talent chord: Flexible, Co-ordinating, Strategic

Quality

You create structure without becoming rigid. You build systems that can flex with change, perfect for dynamic teams or transformation work.

Example: You lead a cross-functional team through a shifting rollout by adjusting timelines without losing sight of the big picture.

Watch out for

Too much flexibility may weaken your leadership signal. Others might feel directionless if you adapt too often.

Example: You adjust priorities so frequently that your team loses track of what matters most.

Coaching tip

Ask yourself: What's flexible, and what must stay firm?

THE GROUNDED VISIONARY
Talent chord: Visionary, Contextual, Responsible

Quality
You think ahead, but with both feet on the ground. You connect future goals to past experience, balancing innovation with accountability.

Example: You lead a digital strategy by first understanding what worked (and didn't) in the last transformation.

Watch out for

You may over-reference the past, or hesitate to take bold leaps.

Example: You question a new idea too long because it doesn't resemble anything that's worked before.

Coaching tip

Ask yourself: What can I carry forward, and what is it time to leave behind?

THE WARM CHALLENGER
Talent chord: Connecting, Competitive, Just

Quality

You challenge people—with care. You fight for fairness and high standards while staying connected and respectful. People trust you to push them.

Example: You give tough feedback to a peer, then help them improve because you want them to succeed.

Watch out for

You may soften your message too much, or push too hard in the name of "standards."

Example: You sugarcoat a conflict to protect the relationship, but the core issue remains unresolved.

Coaching tip

Ask yourself: How can I say what's real and stay connected at the same time?

THE TACTICAL OPTIMIST
Talent chord: Targeted, Trouble-Shooter, Optimistic

Quality

You spot issues early, and believe they can be solved. You move toward challenges with focus, resilience, and a positive mindset.

Example: During a project setback, you reframe it as an opportunity to improve, and bring others back into action.

Watch out for

You may push optimism too far, ignoring warning signs.

Example: You dismiss a teammate's concerns as "negative thinking," missing a crucial risk.

Coaching tip

Ask yourself: What's the best-case scenario, and what do I still need to prepare for?

THE CALM COMMANDER

Talent chord: Confident, Reflective, Mediating

Quality

You lead from stillness. You hold your ground without needing volume. Others listen when you speak, because you rarely speak without purpose.

Example: In a crisis, you pause the noise, reflect, and offer a clear path forward that everyone can follow.

Watch out for

You may be perceived as passive or disengaged when you're actually thinking.

> Example: You're quiet in a meeting, and others misread that as lack of conviction.

Coaching tip

Ask yourself: Where can I show more of what I'm holding inside?

THE CURIOUS BUILDER
Talent chord: Inquiring, Developer, Strategic

Quality

You grow people and ideas. You learn constantly, apply insights, and help others build skills and structures that last.

Example: You set up a mentoring program that develops talent while driving long-term business goals.

Watch out for

You may over-focus on learning and miss the moment to apply.

Example: You attend three webinars on transformation, but never commit to a path for your own team.

Coaching tip

Ask yourself: What do I already know that's ready to be used?

THE EMPOWERING ORGANIZER
Talent chord: Orderly, Inclusive, Developer

Quality
You bring clarity and collaboration. You organize people and systems in a way that lifts others up, not shuts them down.

Example: You redesign onboarding with both structure and space for individual growth.

Watch out for

You may over-structure collaboration and limit natural flow.

Example: You schedule too many "check-ins" and unintentionally reduce autonomy.

Coaching tip

Ask yourself: Where can I organize the outcome—not the process?

THE QUIET NEGOTIATOR

Talent chord: Individualizing, Mediating, Assessing

Quality

You're diplomatic, fair, and tuned into what makes people tick. You balance different needs with subtlety, and help people find common ground.

Example: You navigate a departmental conflict by helping both sides feel heard and respected, leading to real resolution.

Watch out for

You may avoid strong stances or delay decisions while weighing everyone's needs.

> Example: You wait too long to decide on a team lead, trying not to disappoint anyone.

Coaching tip

Ask yourself: What's fair to all, and still clear and timely?

THE STEADY CLIMBER

Talent chord: Responsible, Prominent, Improver

Quality

You grow with consistency. You earn trust through dependability, show up with quiet confidence, and steadily increase your impact.

Example: You take on a stretch assignment, improve the process over time, and earn a key promotion, not by flash, but by follow-through.

Watch out for

You may undervalue visibility or struggle to self-promote.

Example: You do excellent work, but others don't notice because you don't speak about it.

Coaching tip

Ask yourself: Where could I own my impact a little louder?

THE STRUCTURE SHIFTER

Talent chord: Controlling, Flexible, Innovative

Quality

You create systems that evolve. You bring direction and agility, building structure that can flex, not break.

Example: You lead a process redesign that gives clarity and autonomy, adapting weekly based on what's working.

Watch out for

You may shift control too often, or struggle to know when to let go.

> Example: You update the team structure three times in a month, and your team starts to lose focus.

Coaching tip

Ask yourself: What needs stability, and what needs movement?

LEARN TO LISTEN TO OTHERS

When we understand our own chord, we begin to move through work, and life, with more clarity. But we rarely play solo. Most of us work in teams, where different sounds meet and overlap. Some harmonize beautifully. Others clash. And often, we're unaware of what's shaping the dynamic.

This is where real transformation begins: not just in knowing your own sound, but in learning to listen to others.

ABOUT THE AUTHORS

Gitte Justesen is a coach and advisor that helps leaders and talents stand stronger in themselves. Through her expertise in team dynamics, leadership, and diversity, she is focused on bringing real change. Her clients describe her coaching, both individual and in teams, as "a valuable and decisive process" that brings both business breakthroughs and personal transformation.

Josefine Campbell is an executive coach, founder of Campbell Co., and author of POWER BAROMETER and 12 TOOLS FOR MANAGING A SELFISH LEADER. She helps leaders and teams do what they're here to do—with clarity, courage, and honest perspective. Clients include McDonald's, Pandora, and Deloitte. Her work is anchored in real change, not perfection, and inspired by everything that grows wild, including people.

www.ingramcontent.com/pod-product-compliance
Lightning Source LLC
Chambersburg PA
CBHW020927090426
42736CB00010B/1062